1

Hi, I am Uncle Ken Jones, Boandik elder. I am connected to my sea country as well as the land. This is a true story about dolphins. Dolphins and whales are known as **Kaantabul** in my culture. They are very sacred to our people. They help us to catch fish. We protect them because they are very important to us.

Knowledge Books and Software

PORT

# Lincoln Times

Vol. L No. 2713    Established 1927.    $13.00 p.a. (posted)    Single copy 15c.    "Registered at G.P.O., Adelaide, for transmission by post as a newspaper — Category "A".

Port Lincoln, South Australia    Thursday, May 5, 1977

## DRAMA IN THE DARK

The night scene at Memory Cove when the beach was strewn with stranded dolphins, photographed by off-duty police officer Snr. Constable Paul Beresford. Working in white overalls is another off-duty officer, Constable John Potter.

# Volunteers in night battle to save dolphins

A small group of volunteers battled in the dark at Memory Cove last Sunday night to save the lives of 55 dolphins which had run up on the beach that day.

A long and strenuous operation resulted in 41 of the dolphins being successfully refloated.

Divers spoke afterwards of the harrowing experience of hearing stranded dolphins "crying like children" in their distress.

Visitors to the area attempted to rescue some of the dolphins and on return to Port Lincoln reported to the Police who in turn contacted local liaison officer, Mr Ken...

Mr Jones and two off duty St John Ambulance volunteers Paul Beresford and John Potter rushed to Memory Cove and the rescue vehicle arrived at about 8 p.m. and found that the 55 dolphins were all still stranded.

Tickling the smaller ones first, the dolphins were manhandled out to waist deep water with the assistance of an incoming tide, and then directed seawards.

**CONFUSED**

Some were quite placid and co-operative while others were confused and panic stricken.

These had to be redirected several times.

Later at night, National Park Ranger Andrew Spiers from Coffin Bay arrived with two Coffin Bay volunteers, Neville Mattson and John Stenson, to assist in final refloatings.

However, due to the enormity of the task 14 were drowned or collapsed in the sand before rescue could be effected.

Mr Jones said this happened due to suffocation when the weight of their bodies no longer supported the dolphins.

by the water, made it impossible for them to inflate their lungs properly.

He said it had been previously recorded that mass strandings occurred almost always on gently sloping sandy or muddy bottoms.

These were precisely the places where the coastline would fail to give exact echo location information such as the dolphins would get on the steeper rocky parts of the coastline of which Memory Cove is typical.

Abalone divers operating in the area have been notified of increased shark risk.

Two experts from the South Australian Museum arrived on the scene of the stranding yesterday.

They took parts of the dead dolphins for detailed analysis to help determine the reason for the stranding.

It is understood that they found the carcasses low in body fat, which could have been caused either through poor feeding or because they were migrating.

They identified the dolphins as the species commonly known as Bottlenosed Dolphins.

In the Southern part of the beach at Louth Bay on Monday four more stranded dolphins were found dead in shallow water.

These were also identified as Bottle-nosed Dolphins.

One of the dolphins at Louth Bay measured 13 feet.

Mr Jones said today the Santa Rosa, skippered by Tony Santic, picked up floating life rafts and lifeboat.

Mr Jones said all marine mammals including whales, seals and dolphins of every species were protected species under the Fisheries Act 1971-5.

# $200 000 tuna boat sinks

The 58-ft. tuna vessel Zadar sank after suddenly taking water about 12 miles southwest of Williams Island at 4 a.m. last Thursday morning.

The vessel had left Port Lincoln and was heading for the tuna fishing grounds on the continental shelf when the man on watch saw water in the engine room.

He sounded the alarm, but before anything could be done the engine and auxiliary were out of action and there was no power for the pumps.

The owner of Zadar, Mr Ivo Skoljarev, was not on board at the time of the sinking.

On board were the skipper Tony Mislov and Tony Maric, Anton Rnov, Ed Viklink and Bronco Vlasjak.

Mr Skoljarev said Zadar sank within about 20 minutes of the leak being discovered.

**POWER OFF**

Because power was cut off the vessel could not radio for help but her flares were seen by the tuna vessel Alen, skippered by Vince Longin, which picked up the crew.

Another tuna vessel, the Santa Ross, skippered by Frony Santic, picked up the greatest size the species attained.

Mr Jones said he was troubled that his vessel sank in about 45 to 50 fathoms. He said Zadar was valued for insurance at $200,000. He said that when told of the sinking of Zadar he could not at first believe it.

He was deeply grateful to the skipper and crew of the Alen for taking off his crew and to the people who had expressed their sympathy in the loss of his boat.

Mr Skoljarev said he had just purchased equipment to convert Zadar into a prawning vessel after the tuna season.

Last year Zadar was chartered by the South Australian Government for deep sea trawling research.

# INDIAN TEST CRICKETERS TO PLAY HERE

The first match to be played in South Australia by the touring Indian test cricket side at the end of this year will be in Port Lincoln.

At its meeting on Monday night the Port Lincoln City Council had letters from the South Australian Cricket Association and the Port Lincoln Cricket Association informing them of the match.

The date of the match is November 2.

The Indian team is scheduled to fly in to Port Lincoln that morning and depart the same night.

Council agreed to the use of the Centenary Oval for the match.

Port Lincoln was also the venue for the country match played by the last visiting Indian test team.

On that occasion heavy rain prevented play for most of the day.

## WEATHER

Western Agricultural District forecast issued by the bureau at 11.30 a.m. today.

Cool and cloudy fairly generally with a few showers about the coasts and Southern Eyre Peninsula.

Mainly SW to S winds, strong on parts of the coast. Mainly moderate seas.

Outlook for Saturday — coastal drizzle.

In 1976, I was a fisheries officer in Port Lincoln. A message came through saying that some dolphins were stranded at Memory Cove. I thought it might be a trick, but I still had to check it out. I headed off in my 4WD with two local policemen. The road was rough and winding. It took us 4 hours to get there. We arrived at 10pm that night.

Knowledge Books and Software

5

We shone our headlights down the beach and could not believe it! Over 70 bottle-nosed dolphins were stranded. It looked like they had been chasing fish across the cove. When they reached the shallows, their signals got mixed up. Next thing they knew, they were stuck on the sand.

Knowledge Books and Software

7

The big, old dolphins were high up on the sand. They had led the large pod in through the cove and were the first to strand. Further down the beach were the mothers and their calves. They were calling to one another in their own language.

Knowledge Books and Software

Knowledge Books and Software

What could we do? Where do we start? We had no radio or mobile phones back then. There was no-one else around for miles. It was up to the three of us to try and help these sacred animals in any way we could.

Knowledge Books and Software

Knowledge Books and Software

We were lucky it was a cool night. This gave the dolphins a better chance of surviving. The moon was full and bright. This made it easier for us to see. The tide was also coming in. This would make it easier for us to re-float them.

Knowledge Books and Software

**13**

Knowledge Books and Software

We waded all night in the dark, cold water. We pulled the smallest ones out to sea. Many of the young calves would swim straight back to their crying mothers and re-strand. It was a very hard time for them and for us!

Knowledge Books and Software

15

Midnight came and went. We worked hard to drag them back out into deeper water. Time and again, the little ones kept stranding next to their mums. The high tide finally helped us to re-float the mothers. This was important because the calves then stopped re-stranding. They had their mums beside them again.

Knowledge Books and Software

However, there was nothing we could do for those big, old dolphins. They were slowly dying. I have seen a lot of dolphins before, but these were the biggest dolphins I had ever seen. Some of them were almost 4 metres long and had lived in our sea country for many years.

Knowledge Books and Software

Then something happened which I will never forget. While we were dragging the mothers back into deeper water, some of the other mums swam over to us. They turned on their sides as dolphins do. They looked us straight in the eye and they started talking to us. In their language, they were thanking us for saving them and their babies.

Knowledge Books and Software

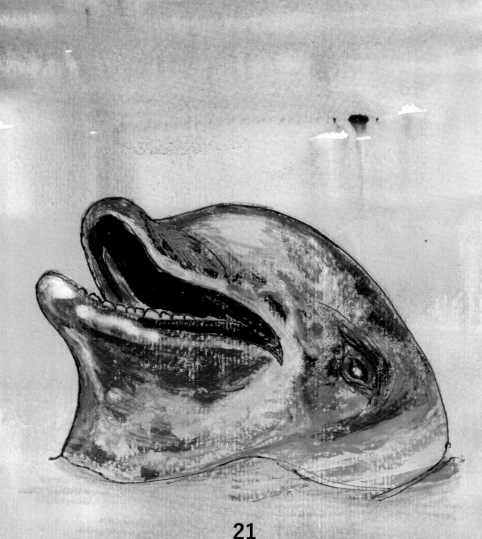

**21**

I will never forget this moment and I still cry when I think about it now. By dawn, we counted 44 rescued dolphins. I wish I could have saved them all, but it just was not possible. Those mother dolphins knew just how we felt. They said thank you in their own language. They knew we were trying to help them, just as they have helped us for many years. Who ever said that dolphins could not talk!

Knowledge Books and Software

23

## Word bank

| | |
|---|---|
| Kaantabul | emotional |
| fisheries | remember |
| Lincoln | carefully |
| policemen | rescued |
| arrived | special |
| signals | |
| grandmothers | |
| calves | |
| language | |
| surviving | |

Knowledge Books and Software